CW00406245

Apache AH-64 Boeing (McDonnell Douglas) 1976–2005

Chris Bishop • Illustrated by Jim Laurier

First published in Great Britain in 2005 by Osprey Publishing
Midland House, West Way, Botley, Oxford OX2 0PH, UK
443 Park Avenue South, New York, NY 10016, USA.
Email: info@ospreypublishing.com

A CIP catalog record for this book is available from the British Library

ISBN 1 84176 016 2

Editor: Katherine Venn
Design: Ken Vail Graphic Design, Cambridge, UK
Index by David Worthington
Originated by PPS Grasmere Ltd, Leeds, UK
Printed in China through World Print Ltd.

05 06 07 08 09   10 9 8 7 6 5 4 3 2 1

For a catalog of all books published by Osprey please contact:

NORTH AMERICA
Osprey Direct, 2427 Bond Street, University Park, IL 60466, USA
E-mail: info@ospreydirectusa.com

ALL OTHER REGIONS
Osprey Direct UK, P.O. Box 140 Wellingborough, Northants, NN8 2FA, UK
E-mail: info@ospreydirect.co.uk

www.ospreypublishing.com

Artist's note

Readers may care to note that copies of the artwork used in this title are
available for private sale. All reproduction copyright whatsoever is retained by
the Publishers. All inquiries should be addressed to:

Jim Laurier, 85 Carroll Street, Keene, New Hampshire 03431, USA

The Publishers regret that they can enter into no correspondence upon this
matter.

Editor's note

Interview with LtCol William Bryan originally published in *Gulf Air War Debrief*
(London: 1991), courtesy of Aerospace Publishing.

APACHE AH-64 BOEING (MCDONNELL DOUGLAS) 1976–2005

INTRODUCTION

In the early hours of January 17, 1991, Lieutenant Tom Drew thumbed the radio switch in the pilot's seat of his AH-64A Apache and announced "Party in ten." Ten seconds later, at 0238 local time, eight helicopters of Task Force Normandy, detached from the 101st Airborne Division, launched Hellfire missiles, followed by rockets and gunfire. Their targets were two key air-defense radar sites inside Iraq.

The first shots of Operation *Desert Storm* had been fired, not by US Air Force F-117 Stealth fighters or Tomahawk cruise missiles from naval vessels in the Persian Gulf, but by a small force of Army helicopters. Flying north out of Al Jouf in Saudi Arabia and across the Iraqi border, Task Force Normandy's Apaches had made a supremely effective and deadly accurate attack that was to become the norm for subsequent AH-64 operations during the war against Iraq.

Still regarded as the world's premier attack helicopter a quarter of a century after its first flight, the AH-64 Apache proved itself to be one of the world's great combat aircraft during the first Gulf War. After

Twenty years after the first production AH-64A Apache was rolled out, on September 30, 1983, the AH-64D Apache Longbow maintains the Apache's reputation as the most deadly combat helicopter in the world and continues successfully to meet the needs of the US Army and other armies around the world. (Boeing)

undertaking the first attack mission of Operation *Desert Storm*, the Apache was to go on to destroy many Iraqi positions before it began to operate in the mission for which it was designed – to support the troops on the ground, and to destroy enemy armor.

The AH-64 Apache was designed as an Army weapon. The attack helicopter has become the main antiarmor platform in modern warfare, replacing the antitank guns of World War Two and the 1950s. Its versatility also enables the helicopter to stand in for field artillery when providing fire support to ground forces – indeed, the first gunships were known as aerial rocket artillery.

While it is never going to win any beauty contest, the Apache's bug-like silhouette nevertheless supports a highly effective weapons system. It has a devastating punch with its Hellfire missiles, air-to-ground rockets and M230 Chain Gun. This arsenal is directed by an array of high-tech sensors. Although occasionally fragile, and sometimes difficult to maintain in the field, the Apache's television, infrared, and radar "eyes" can pinpoint a target under almost any weather conditions, by day or by night.

Like an infantryman, the Apache uses a combination of stealth, agility, and speed of movement to enhance its fighting prowess. It can hide, duck, rise, and fight in a fluid, fast-changing environment. It combines the capabilities of an infantry squad with that of the tank and artillery, using fire-and-maneuver tactics at close quarters while at the same time being able to reach out and destroy targets at ranges of several miles with its advanced and highly accurate weaponry.

BELOW LEFT **Criticized in its early days as being too complex and too expensive for operational use, the original AH-64A Apache proved itself as a weapon system second to none in the only place that matters – in combat. The Apache was one of the star performers of the first Gulf War, and it has since seen successful action all over the world.** (McDonnell Douglas)

BELOW RIGHT **The Apache is the backbone of the US Army's aviation combat force. In service since 1983, it has seen considerable action since its combat debut in Panama at the end of the 1980s, but the mission for which it was designed was to be used *en masse* in the destruction of Soviet armored units – should the unthinkable have happened, and the Cold War turned "Hot."** (TRH Pictures)

DEVELOPMENT

The Apache was conceived and developed at the height of the Cold War. The West needed an answer to the Group of Soviet Forces in Germany, seemingly poised with their Warsaw Pact allies just over the inner German frontier. That apparent threat presented the main challenge to NATO's planners, whose worst nightmare was a sudden armored attack by tens of thousands of Soviet tanks across the North German plain and through the Fulda Gap.

The Apache was optimized to detect tanks from a considerable distance and to kill them. The helicopter was expected to fight in a highly mobile fashion, keeping low and using the terrain and vegetation for cover. Popping out of cover, it could acquire a target and fire within seconds, ducking back into hiding once its missiles were away, remaining well beyond the range of the enemy's weapons. Even if things were to go wrong, the Apache was more heavily protected than any previous helicopter and could use its weapons and maneuverability in a short-range fight.

The Apache is a formidable weapon, but it was not the first of its kind. As a combat aircraft for army use, it was preceded by the Bell AH-1 Huey Cobra from the Vietnam years. The Huey Cobra had a highly successful combat career in Vietnam after its introduction in August 1967. The Hughes BGM-71 TOW (Tube-launched, Optically-tracked, Wire-guided) missile ultimately gave the sleek "Snake" unprecedented hitting power against armored targets, coupled with secure stand-off ranges.

In Europe, where the "real" war would be fought, the arrival of the AH-1 paved the way for the second generation of US attack helicopters that would be firmly dedicated to killing Soviet tanks in Germany. However, the AH-1 was originally only a stop-gap – developed in haste to cover delays in the Army's "big plan" for armed helicopters.

After the successful debut of armed UH-1 utility helicopters in Vietnam, and before the equally successful introduction of the Cobra, the US Army initiated the Advanced Aerial Fire Support System program to develop a new combat helicopter for gunship, escort, and fire support tasks. The result was a 1966 contract with Lockheed to develop the AH-56A Cheyenne. It was conceived not as a maneuverable armed helicopter for nap-of-the-earth (NoE) flying, but as a large weapons platform for Vietnam-era gun and missile attacks. The Cheyenne had a General Electric T64 turboshaft driving a four-bladed main rotor, coupled with a conventional tail rotor and a decidedly unconventional pusher propeller at the end of the tailboom.

The first AH-56A made its maiden flight on September 21, 1967, and in trials achieved a startling maximum speed of 220 knots (253mph). In January 1968 the US Department of Defense signed a contract for an initial batch of 375. However, the Air Force was vehemently opposed to Army plans for acquiring this advanced helicopter, claiming that its close-support mission should be the responsibility of Air Force fixed-wing machines.

The first prototype crashed on March 12, 1969, killing the pilot. The advanced nature of the machine meant that technical delays and hitches abounded. However, the development that killed the project was the advent and worldwide distribution of the shoulder-launched SAM, in the shape of the SA-7 "Grail" (Soviet designation 9K32 Strela-2). It was

ABOVE **Far and away the most advanced helicopter of its time, the Lockheed AH-56A Cheyenne was a rotary-winged equivalent of a ground-attack fighter, with much the same capability. However, it was extremely complex and painfully expensive, and its vulnerability to the new hand-held SAMs being introduced in the late 1960s saw the project cancelled. (TRH Pictures)**

clear that, to survive over the battlefields of the 1970s, any new helicopter would have to operate at less than tree-top height and be supremely agile. What was needed was a gunboat and not a heavy cruiser, and so the US Army retired to generate another specification.

The space left by the cancellation of what might have been up to 1,000 Cheyennes still needed to be filled. With an eye on the Central European front, the US Army's next requirement coalesced around an aircraft that would better the AH-1 in terms of range, performance and firepower while still being maneuverable enough to fly NoE missions through, around, and under forests, hills, and power lines. The AH-1/TOW combination was still the best available and held the line in Europe for a decade, but it obviously could be improved.

In August 1972 the official Request for Proposals (RFP) for the Advanced Attack Helicopter (AAH) was announced. It specified an aircraft that would cruise at 145 knots (167mph) with a full load of eight TOW missiles (or a minimum expendable ordnance load of 1,000lb) for a mission duration of 1.9 hours. Performance demands were set, surprisingly, in what were effectively Middle Eastern terms: 4,000ft altitude at an ambient temperature of 95°F (35°C). By way of comparison, conditions for "NATO hot day" operations were defined as 2,000ft at 70°F (21°C). Maximum speed was to be 175 knots (201mph) and maximum vertical rate of climb 500ft/min.

The new helicopter would have to have operational g limits of +3.5 and -1.5 and be able to resist hits from 12.7mm armor-piercing incendiary rounds. In addition, the rotorhead (and the entire aircraft) had to remain flyable after a hit from a 23mm high-explosive incendiary shell, the then standard Warsaw Pact antiaircraft artillery (AAA) caliber. A sign of the prescience of these requirements is that they would not be seen as unreasonable, or inadequate, today.

ABOVE **Air Vehicle 02 fires a salvo of FFAR (Folding-Fin Aerial Rockets) during a test flight in the late 1970s. AV-02, the first Apache to fly, displays the high-mounted tailplane that was to be changed to a low-mounted "stabilator" on pre-production and production aircraft, introduced partly to save weight. (TRH Pictures)**

The SAM threat to the aircraft was perhaps even a higher priority and the AAH would have to prove that its infrared (IR) signature, and thus its vulnerability to shoulder-launched infantry SAMs, could be reduced to an acceptably low level. Such passive counter-measures would be backed up by chaff/flare dispensers. Crew survivability was placed at a premium, as the inherent fragility of the helicopter meant that far too many crews had been lost in Vietnam.

Of course, the key to survivability on the battlefield would be to allow the AAH to kill its targets outside the air defense envelope that could be expected around an advancing armored column. The alarming Israeli experience of the 1973 Yom Kippur War showed that this might no longer be possible when faced with Soviet weapons such as the ZSU-23-4 Shilka radar-directed mobile AAA system or SA-6 "Gainful", SA-8 "Gecko" and SA-9 "Gaskin" mobile SAMs. The TOW missile was becoming progressively less effective against these defenses, and its use of wire-guidance left the launch aircraft exposed for an unacceptable length of time.

Designed initially by Hughes (which was later absorbed by McDonnell Douglas, which was itself taken over by Boeing), the Apache had a protracted development history as it encountered both technical and financial troubles. Five competing submissions were made for the new helicopter – from Bell, Boeing-Vertol (teamed with Grumman Aérospace), Hughes, Lockheed, and Sikorsky. Bell Helicopter Textron, not surprisingly, saw itself as the front-runner. It had amassed the most relevant experience of any of the competitors and its resultant YAH-63 (Bell Model 409) had the appearance of a thoroughbred. Hughes' designers developed the angular and awkward-looking Model 77, which, to the US Army, became the YAH-64.

On June 22, 1973, the US Department of Defense announced that the Bell YAH-63 and Hughes YAH-64 had been chosen as the AAH competitors. This launched Phase 1 of the competition, whereby both firms would build and fly two prototypes, plus a Ground Test Vehicle (GTV), for a competitive fly-off. By June 1975, Hughes had begun ground tests with AV-01 (Air Vehicle-01) the prototype. This aircraft would be tasked with all the preliminary power tests, but AV-02 would be the first to fly. In fact, AV-01 never flew and served as Hughes' *de facto* GTV. By contrast, Bell had already run a dedicated YAH-63 GTV in April of that year and its apparent lead in the program forced Hughes to hurriedly

LEFT **Hughes Helicopters proposed the Model 77 in response to an Army request for a dedicated attack helicopter. Although only a mockup, the design featured many of the characteristics that would emerge on the AH-64 Apache. (TRH Pictures)**

accelerate its work. The first YAH-64 succeeded in beating the YAH-63 into the air by one day, making its first take-off on September 30, 1975.

An intensive flight test program was undertaken, first by the manufacturers and then by the US Army. During this period, the TOW missile armament originally planned for the AAH was replaced by the Rockwell Hellfire (HELicopter-Launched, FIRE-and-forget), a laser-guided antitank missile that promised effective engagement ranges in excess of 3.7 miles, or double that of the TOW.

On December 10, 1976, having reviewed the evaluation results, the Secretary of the Army announced that the Hughes YAH-64 was the winner of the AAH competition. Hughes had encountered some problems during the Phase 1 evaluation, resulting in a redesign of the rotor system. The mast was lengthened and the blade tips were swept back. The weight of the prototype also had to be reduced and this was achieved by redesigning the tail unit and by introducing lightweight Black Hole IR suppressors.

The Phase 2 contract called for the building of three production standard AH-64s, conversion of the two prototypes and GTV to production standard, and complete weapons and sensor system integration. The first flight of the modified AV-02, by now in production configuration, took place on November 28, 1977. Hellfire tests began in April 1979. Two competing TADS/PNVS (Target Acquisition and Designation Sight/Pilot's Night Vision Sensor) systems were installed on the AH-64 prototypes, AV-02 carrying Martin-Marietta's system and AV-03 being equipped with the Northrop design.

The last of the Phase 2 batch of three aircraft, AV-06, flew on March 16, 1980. This was the first to fly with the definitive "stabilator" design and extended tail rotor. In April 1980 a crucial landmark in the AAH story was reached, with the selection of the Martin-Marietta TADS/PNVS for production. Sadly, 1980 ended on a tragic note. On November 20, AV-04 departed on a routine tail incidence/drag test, accompanied by a T-28D photo chase plane. Flying in close formation, the two collided, and only the pilot of the T-28 survived. In May 1981, AV-02, 03 and 06 were handed over to the US Army, in preparation for the AH-64's final Operational Test II (OTII) evaluation at Fort Hunter-Liggett, which was successful.

One change decided on after OTII was the move to an uprated version of the T700 engine, the T700-GE-701, rated at 1,690shp (1,259kW). It was during the final stages of AAH Phase 2 testing, late in 1981, that the name "Apache" was adopted, in keeping with the US Army's tradition of giving

Native American tribal names to its helicopter types.

It was not until April 15, 1982, that the full-scale go-ahead for Apache production was finally given. The US Army had increased its Apache requirement to 536 aircraft, but was then forced by Congressional financial constraints to cut this back to 446. On this basis, Hughes estimated the total program cost would be $5,994 million. The US Army had always accepted that the unit cost would creep up from $1.6 million (in 1972 dollars), but was now faced with a price per aircraft of over $13 million (rising to $16.2 million later that year). However, even though the AAH was faced with serious political opposition, the Apache had powerful friends. A letter dated July 22, 1982, was sent by General Bernard C. Rogers, NATO Supreme Commander in Europe, to the Apache's chief detractors in the Senate. Rogers' letter spelled out the threat to Europe posed by the Warsaw Pact and its massive tank inventory, and stressed the urgent need for a counter. It ended with the words, "we need the AH-64 in Europe *now* and we cannot afford the luxury of another trip to the drawing board."

ABOVE **The official handover to the US Army of the first production AH-64A took place on September 30, 1983. A final total of 827 AH-64As (including six prototypes) were built, the bulk of that production being delivered to the Army between 1983 and 1990. (McDonnell Douglas)**

The first Apache for the US Army was rolled out in a ceremony held at the Hughes works at Mesa, AZ, ahead of schedule, on September 30, 1983. It was eight years to the day after the first flight. The stated price of the aircraft (its "over-the-fence" cost according to the then-Project Manager Brigadier Charles Drenz) was $7.8 million in 1984 terms or $9 million in real-year terms. This equated to a unit cost of approximately $14 million when development costs were included, making the Apache far and away the most expensive production helicopter up to that time. Hughes planned to accelerate production to a peak of 12 per month by 1986, with purchases of 144 AH-64s in FY85 followed by a projected 144 in FY86 and 56 in FY87.

Production Vehicle 01 (PV-01) made its 30-minute maiden flight on January 9, 1984. By then, the prototype fleet had logged over 4,500 hours in the air. However, this event had been upstaged in the headlines by the announcement, three days earlier, that Hughes Helicopters was about to become a subsidiary of McDonnell Douglas.

AH-64B

The AH-64B was to have been the first interim upgrade of the Apache design. Introduced in

1991 after Operation *Desert Storm*, it was proposed to improve 254 AH-64As by fitting a Global Positioning System (GPS), new radios, new rotor blades, and improved navigation systems. The new secure communications system was designed to allow the AH-64B to hand off targets to other platforms. In November 1991 Congress authorized more than $82 million for AH-64 Apache modifications, as proposed in the President's budget. Congress stated that the purpose of this funding was to initiate Apache-B modifications, including improvements that had been approved as a result of combat experience in the Gulf. Congress expected that when the more extensive AH-64C enhancements were approved, the Apache modification program would switch from "B" conversions to the newer upgrade. However, the "B" program was cancelled in 1992.

AH-64C

Late in 1991 Congress authorized an additional $11 million for the implementation of a plan to "skip" the AH-64B model and move on to an AH-64B+ configuration. In November 1991 Congress agreed to provide an additional $21 million for a program to upgrade the AH-64 to a "C" configuration – in essence, all of the modifications then being considered for the definitive Apache upgrade, the Longbow (see below), minus the T-800 engine and the mast-mounted radar.

Key to the Apache's success from its earliest days in US Army service was the incorporation of a helmet-mounted display: anywhere the pilot looked, the TADS/PNVS turret in the nose followed, projecting an image through a monocular on the pilot's or (as in this case) the gunner's helmet. (McDonnell Douglas)

None of these funds could be released until the Secretary of Defense submitted to the House and Senate Appropriations Committees an AH-64 modification master plan and schedule, with budget, and certified that this program was fully funded through fiscal years 1993–1998.

Approximately 540 Apaches were to be upgraded to AH-64C standard, but the designation was abandoned after 1993. Although the designation was dropped, the plan was not, and as of 2001 it was decided that only about half the 501 AH-64A Apaches that were to be upgraded to the AH-64D configuration would eventually receive the full upgrade, even though all were to be designated AH-64D.

Longbow

The AH-64D Longbow Apache is the ultimate development of America's most important attack helicopter program to date. US Army pilots have described the Longbow as a helicopter from the next generation.

Since the earliest days of AH-64A operations there have been plans to upgrade the helicopter. In the mid-1980s, even as the first Apaches were entering service, McDonnell Douglas began studies of the Advanced/Apache Plus, which was later referred to, unofficially, as the "AH-64B." The AH-64B would have had a revised, updated cockpit with a new fire control system, Stinger air-to-air missiles, and a redesigned Chain Gun. Aimed exclusively at the US Army, the program was abandoned before it reached the hardware stage.

A ground crewman loads the rocket pods of an AH-64D Longbow Apache with an inert, practice air-to-air missile. Apaches have carried Sidewinder, Stinger, and Matra Mistral missiles, and are currently being tested with an air-to-air variant of the British Starstreak high-velocity man-portable SAM. (Boeing)

With new technologies becoming available, there was now the possibility of transforming the already formidable Apache into something of even greater capability. Operational limitations with the AH-64A became apparent during *Desert Storm* and provided the stimulus for developing an improved attack variant.

One of the "new" Apache's most significant developments was the mounting of a Longbow radar above the rotorhead to provide millimeter-wave (MMW) guidance for specially developed "fire-and-forget" AGM-114L Hellfire missiles. When this was fully integrated into the helicopter's systems, the AH-64D was renamed the Longbow Apache. Largely impervious to atmospheric interference, the mast-mounted Longbow radar system allows the AH-64D to launch all 16 AGM-114L Hellfire missiles while remaining hidden behind a tree-line. Thus, in wartime, the Longbow Apache can stay concealed while attacking targets, thereby increasing its chances of surviving retaliation from AAA or shoulder-launched SAMs.

A pair of AH-64D Apaches fly at low level over the desert. The aircraft in the rear is a Longbow Apache, fitted with a mast-mounted millimetric radar system. The standard AH-64D in front has been equipped with all of the Longbow's upgrades barring the radar system. It can be upgraded to full Longbow configuration in four hours. (Boeing)

Although the radar system is probably the most important change in a tactical sense, the Longbow Apache has been significantly upgraded in other areas. The AH-64D has been fitted with a totally new avionics system. Four dual-channel MIL-STD 1553B data buses combine with new processors and an uprated electrical system to greatly increase the capabilities of the AH-64D compared to the AH-64A. The cockpit of the original Apache was a confusing mass of dials and more than 1,200 switches: in the Longbow cockpit these have been replaced by a Litton Canada multi-function display, two 6in square color CRT displays from Allied Signal Aerospace, and just 200 switches.

An AH-64D Apache Longbow equipped with the Modernized Target Acquisition Designation Sight/Pilot Night Vision Sensor (M-TADS/PNVS) lifts off on the first test flight of the new system. The M-TADS/PNVS provides a 150 percent improvement in performance and reliability over its predecessor. (Boeing)

Improved helmet-mounted displays, an upgraded Plessey AN/ASN-157 Doppler navigation system, and Honeywell AN/APN-209 radar altimeter have also been incorporated. In service the AH-64D will have a dual embedded GPS and inertial navigation fit plus new secure VHF/FM radios. The helicopter's improved navigation suite gives it near all-weather capability – the original Apache-A was more accurately described as having adverse-weather capability. The larger volume of avionics needing to be crammed into the Longbow has forced the designers to expand the size of the Apache's cheek fairings, which have become known as EFABs (Enhanced Forward Avionics Bays).

The fluid nature of the battlefield has seen communication between friendly forces play an increasingly important role. Incorporating a data transfer module (DTM), the AH-64D is able to talk not only to other AH-64Ds and OH-58Ds, but also to USAF C3I assets such as the Rivet-Joint RC-135 and the J-STARS E-8. Target information can be supplied to the Longbow Apache crew on a secure frequency, allowing them to be directed safely into an assigned "killing zone." Once the attack has begun, the Longbow radar can catalog targets, designating those that are deemed to be the most threatening.

The Apache's current General Electric T700-GE-701 turboshafts are to be completely replaced by uprated 1,723shp (1,285kW) T700-GE-701C engines. The more powerful 701C has already been standard on existing AH-64As (from the 604th production aircraft, delivered in 1990, onwards) and has proved to deliver a marked increase in performance.

The US Defense Acquisition Board authorized a 51-month AH-64D development program in August 1990. This was later extended to 70 months to incorporate integration of the AGM-114L Hellfire missile. Full-scale production of 232 Longbows was authorized on October 13, 1995, with the complete US Army AH-64D contract also calling for 13,311 AGM-114L missiles. The first AH-64Ds were delivered in March 1997, with the first front line unit becoming operational in July 1998.

Echoing the reaction to the original Apache in the late 1970s, the AH-64D was criticized by many observers as being too complex, too expensive, and potentially unreliable. But the Longbow's capability was validated spectacularly in a series of field tests carried out between January 30 and February 9, 1995, at China Lake. In the tests, a joint team of AH-64As and AH-64Ds undertook gunnery trials involving some of the most complex exercise scenarios ever devised. The test results were staggering. The AH-64Ds achieved 300 confirmed enemy armor kills, as compared to the AH-64As, which notched up just 75. Four AH-64Ds were deemed to have been shot down, as opposed to 28 AH-64As. One test official stated, "In all my years of testing, I have never seen a test system which could so dominate the system it is intended to replace."

The Apache's Hellfire missiles enable the helicopter to destroy any main battle tank currently in service. Current model Hellfires have a tandem warhead designed to defeat the layered defenses carried by many of the latest armored vehicles. (US Army)

Apache weapons

The Apache's weapons are divided into two tactical categories: point weapons and area weapons. Hellfire provides point-attack capability and is the key to the AH-64's success as a tank-killer. The AGM-114C Hellfire is the current base model in Army service. It has a semi-active laser seeker and an improved low-visibility detection capability, compared to the original A model. The AGM-114C also flies a flatter trajectory to the target, and is equipped with a low-smoke motor to minimize the risk that potential targets see the incoming missile in time to initiate countermeasures.

The AGM-114F has a tandem warhead for use against reactive armor. The AGM-114K Hellfire II was developed as a result of Gulf War experience. A new autopilot works by regulating launch speed, allowing a

Hellfire allows the Apache to make precision attacks on armor: its M230 Chain Gun can destroy soft targets with equal precision. Apaches carry a varied ammunition load depending on the mission: for antiarmor missions it will only carry 320 rounds, but for close-support or escort it will carry up to 1,200 rounds. (TRH Pictures)

steeper terminal dive. The AGM-114K's seeker has been improved to overcome backscatter interference. The latest Hellfire is believed to have a maximum range in excess of the 8,750yd range quoted for earlier versions. Hellfire has been extensively tested on the battlefield, especially during Operation *Desert Storm*. When used against Iraqi armor the striking power of Hellfire was absolute – a single Hellfire strike would destroy any target, as long as it remained within the limits of the engagement envelope.

The Apache's primary area weapon system is the 2.75in (70mm) Hydra 70 rocket. Rockets are carried in 19-round pods, although a seven-round pod is also available. The basic Hydra warhead is the M151 High-Explosive (HE) round, used for antipersonnel and antimaterial tasks. The M261 HE multi-purpose submunition (MPSM) warhead can be used against light armor and carries nine M73 grenade-sized submunitions. The M255E1 flechette warhead contains 1,180 hardened steel flechettes and is primarily an antipersonnel/soft target weapon.

The M230 30mm Chain Gun cannon is the Apache's secondary area weapon, owing to its relatively short range. Using aluminum-cased ammunition, the Apache can carry approximately 1,200 rounds – 1,100 in the magazine and 90 in place on the chain feed to the gun. The M230 has a maximum rate of fire of 600–650 rounds per minute and "spools up" to this rate in just 0.2 seconds.

According to Colonel William Bryan of the 101st Airborne Division, interviewed soon after the end of Operation *Desert Storm*:

Hellfire is for point targets, something hard that has to be engaged with a precision munition with a lot of penetration. This laser-guided missile will hit targets at ranges of more than 3 miles. How much further, I'm not allowed to say. The 2.75 is a good area weapon if you have a lot of vehicles or personnel in a small area, and can strike from about 5 or 6 miles. Each rocket can contain nine sub-munitions, which were found to be extremely effective against trucks. The Chain Gun is in between. It is extremely accurate and will penetrate light armor if you are within 1.2 miles.

An AH-64D Apache prototype launches a Hellfire missile during field tests. The Hellfire used in the Longbow Apache can lock on to a target indicated by the helicopter's radar, but it can also be used in full "fire-and-forget" mode: launched towards a specific coordinate, the missile searches for and locks on to a target while in flight. (Boeing)

APACHE IN ACTION

Apaches perform their task of killing targets with finesse, despite certain limitations. The long, slender Apache with its gunner and pilot in a two- seat, tandem cockpit offers excellent handling and flying characteristics and good visibility. The helicopter responds well to a skilled hand at the controls and performs as well as any battlefield helicopter in service anywhere. On the ground, its wheeled undercarriage affords easy movement for maintenance.

The original Apache lacked global-positioning (GPS) and terrain-following systems for navigation on long missions and, though these are standard on the AH-64D, many older aircraft have yet to be retrofitted. As a product of the 1970s, the Apache is an analog, not a digital warrior. Mission planning for any Apache mission is arduous because every eventuality must be foreseen, sketched out and planned on paper before the aircraft are in the air. Apaches fight as a team and, if the cohesion of that team is lost, so is the mission. Apache crews know the truth of Clausewitz's maxim that "no plan survives contact with the enemy." Communication of new ideas or intelligence is nearly impossible after launch, so until the late 1990s Apache crews have had to fly and fight in a stressful combat environment hoping that all the answers have been worked out before the shooting starts. All that has changed, however, with the entry into service of the Longbow Apache.

The attack helicopter battalion is an instrument of precise firepower, with the maneuverability to mass combat power at a decisive time, yet one which always works as part of a combined arms team. The Apache is tasked with nine primary missions:

> to attack massed armor or light formations
> to attack in depth to extend the influence of its own land forces
> to dominate avenues of approach
> to reinforce ground forces by fire
> to defeat enemy penetrations
> to protect the flanks of a friendly force – be it on the move or static
> to provide security for the movement and passage of lines by ground forces
> to conduct reconnaissance
> to conduct search-and-attack missions

Offensive operations

The Apache's role in offensive missions is categorized in several ways. The first of these is a "movement to contact", which is to gain or re-establish contact with the enemy, though not necessarily to engage it. Engagements from a movement to contact should be against targets of opportunity, or through chance rather than design. The primary function of a movement to contact is to place the Apache battalion in a secure position to conduct its pre-planned attack. Those attacks are sub-divided into two categories: "hasty" and "deliberate". A hasty attack takes advantage of an enemy's weakness or sustains the momentum of the main attacking force. A deliberate attack is conducted against an enemy that is well organized and cannot be turned or bypassed. It will be pre-planned and briefed using all the intelligence, and time, available.

After a successful attack comes "exploitation," to prevent the enemy from regrouping or withdrawing. The attack helicopter battalion (ATKHB) will still be operating as part of a larger force and will attempt to strike the flank and rear of the enemy force. Then comes the "pursuit," in which the Apache ATKHB will leave flank and contact engagement to the

The two-man cockpit of the Apache follows the pattern established by Bell for the pioneering Model 209 Cobra, with the pilot behind and above the weapons operator. The Apache differs from its predecessor, however, in being provided with much more armor protection for its crew. (Westland)

ground forces and, instead, strike deep to cut off the retreating enemy force and block any relieving forces. This calls for very precise and well-planned coordination between friendly forces.

The two forms of defensive operations that concern the ATKHB are "area" and "mobile" operations. ATKHBs conduct area defense in terrain where the enemy has a mobility advantage and must be denied avenues of approach or specific areas. A mobile defense allows the enemy to advance to a point where it is vulnerable to attack by two subdivided units, one to contain the advancing force and one to destroy it.

Task Force Normandy, the AH-64A attack on Iraqi radar sites close to the Saudi border in January 1991, was a classic example of an ATKHB "deep" operation. It was an attack mission directed against forces not currently engaged but which shaped the outcome of future events. Although such deep penetration operations can incur high risks, they can deliver an equally high payoff if undertaken successfully.

Into combat

The AH-64A proved its capabilities in action during Operation *Desert Storm*, but it actually saw action for the first time just over a year before, when 160 Army helicopters took part in Operation *Just Cause*, the American operation against General Noriega's Panamanian government, which began in December 1989. Apaches self-deployed from the United States to make their combat debut. The AH-64 provided effective fire support, engaging several targets that were dangerously close to friendly units. Although the Apache exhibited some mechanical problems during *Just Cause*, it performed well for such an advanced attack aircraft being used operationally for the first time. The AH-64's advanced sensors and sighting systems were effective against Panamanian government forces. Lieutenant General Carl Stiner, commander of the XVIII Airborne Corps, was quoted as observing that the Apache could "fire a Hellfire missile through a window five miles away – and it could do it at night."

Apache helicopters played a key role in this action, where much of the activity took place at night. Operations in Panama showed that, when equipped with state-of-the-art night vision and targeting devices, Army aviators equipped with the AH-64 did indeed "own the night." Successful though the Apache was in Panama, it was to gain even greater glory less than a year later, when the AH-64 was to play an important part in the liberation of Kuwait.

Gulf War

On November 20, 1990, the 11th Aviation Brigade was alerted for deployment to Southwest Asia from Storck Barracks in Illesheim, Germany. The first elements arrived in theater November 24, 1990. By January 15, 1991, the unit had moved 147 helicopters, 325 vehicles, and 1,476 soldiers to the region.

On January 17, 1991, four MH-53 Pave Low III helicopters from the 20th Special Operations Squadron led two flights of Apaches to make the first strike of the war. Pilots of the eight AH-64A Apache attack helicopters of 101st Airborne Division (Air Assault) fired the first shots of Operation *Desert Storm*. Code-named "Normandy," in remembrance of the 101st "Screaming Eagles" role in the liberation of Europe during the Second World War, the dangerous mission consisted of simultaneous attacks designed to knock out two key early-warning radar installations in western Iraq at precisely 0238 hours, January 17, 1991. Both radar sites, each hit by a team of four Apaches, were destroyed in less than five minutes. Each pilot's primary target became the secondary target for adjacent Apache team members.

The Apache crews observed a radio blackout until ten seconds before unleashing up to 27 Hellfire missiles that destroyed 16 to 18 targets at each site. The near-perfect mission opened a 20-mile-wide corridor all the way into Baghdad, Iraq. Within minutes, over 100 US Air Force jets streaked across the border for the undetected bombing

attacks on key Iraqi targets that marked the start o Operation *Desert Storm's* punishing air war. By th end of the day 900 coalition aircraft had passe through the corridor.

A total of 277 US Army Apaches took pa in the lightning 100-hour ground war. Most o the Apache's earlier mechanical problems ha been corrected and whatever doubts remaine regarding its durability and combat effectivene were quickly dispelled. During the conflict AH-64 were credited with destroying more than 500 tank plus hundreds of armored personnel carrier trucks, and other vehicles. Apaches als demonstrated the ability to perform when calle upon, logging thousands of combat hours : readiness rates in excess of 85 percent during th Gulf War.

Lieutenant Colonel William Bryan, of the 2 Battalion/229th Aviation Regiment, interviewe after the end of hostilities, recalled what it was like t fly the AH-64 in Gulf War combat:

Although Apaches traditionally operate as part of a team with scout helicopters, the addition of the Longbow radar means that the AH-64D can do its own scouting by day or by night, using newly fitted data links to provide instant information for unit commanders to the rear. (McDonnell Douglas)

Ten days prior to G Day, the Coalition offensive on February 24, the Apache battalions of the 101st began flying armed reconnaissance missions into Iraq. On occasion we went as deep as 93 miles into hostile territory.

We even began to take prisoners, the first attack helicopter unit ever to do so. About 62 miles into Iraq, we found an infantry battalion astride a road that units of the 101st were planning to use on G Day. We went in at first light, and began to work the position, using 30mm cannon and 2.75in rockets. The Air Force worked in some air strikes.

After we had been engaged for about five hours, we got a leaflet team to drop leaflets, and an Arabic speaker told them over a PA set that if they surrendered they would be given safe passage and would not be harmed. Once some surrendered, the rest began to follow. There were 476 of them! We alerted the brigade Chinook battalion and brought in eight CH-47s to haul them back to captivity.

We knew that on G Day, the division was going to establish an airhead very deep inside Iraq, so in the week before that my mission was reconnaissance, to check the route into the country, destroy fortifications and clear the zone of enemy forces. Division's sector was 31 miles wide and 124 miles deep. On G Day, the division moved along pre-selected air routes to an operating base 93 miles inside Iraq. We had the base up and running within eight hours.

Our sector was far to the west of the main Iraqi troop concentrations. It was lightly defended and lightly populated. We reached the Euphrates, about 31 miles north of the forward base, that first day. The Iraqis we did see tried to run to the north. Once they saw the Apaches they would leave their vehicles and take cover. We then destroyed the vehicles.

We did not use the OH-58s with which we were normally paired as air scouts. In the desert, there is no problem with target acquisition. The human eyeball can see for up to 20 miles, maybe even more with the dust signatures that helicopters and vehicles throw up. The traditional scout role, which is acquiring targets, is not needed. In any case the OH-58 does not have the kind of navigation system we do. The Apaches did their own scouting and attacking, with the OH-58s following up behind, coordinating with artillery and air strikes and providing air defense with their Stinger heat-seeking missiles.

When we came across a convoy, I would attack with one of the battalion's three companies. As the attack progressed I had one company attacking, one about 20 miles back in a holding area, and one 30 miles back at the FARP (Forward Area Refueling Point) at the forward operating base. That way there was one company conducting the engagement, one company at the holding area about five or ten minutes' flight time away and the third company refueling and rearming. There might only have been a third of the people up there, but the enemy was being engaged continuously.

Companies normally operate in two teams. The light team of two Apaches will usually be the first to engage, covered by the heavy team of three or four helicopters. Then the heavy team will take up the fight.

Our greatest concerns were the Iraqi shoulder-fired SAMs. We could get around the sophisticated long-range systems by flying at low altitude and letting the ground clutter mask our signature. But with the man-pack SAMs, one person in a hole in the ground can take you out. We also knew that the enemy had over 5,000 armored vehicles, each with a heavy antiaircraft machine-gun and he had large numbers of 23mm and 57mm cannon. As long as we stayed 1.8 miles away we were generally out of range though, and in any case we were flying at 25ft or less.

In the desert, you couldn't hide behind the terrain. It should have been extremely dangerous, since some of their SAM systems outranged us, but the Iraqis showed little or no desire to fight. They had the equipment, but they didn't have the resolve.

Had the Iraqis been an armored force we would have made stand-off attacks, but in this case we shot them with cannon fire to get them stopped and the people dismounted. Then we fired three Hellfires, which took out the three lead vehicles. From that point on we were able to finish them off with 30mm and 2.75in rockets.

We flew a number of joint attack teams with USAF A-10s and F-16s. If we found a target we would contact the Air Liaison Officer (ALO). As fighters arrived on station they would report to the ALO. He would assign fighters to missions, giving the USAF guys our frequency.

He'd talk to us direct for a briefing on where to attack. Sometimes we laser-designated for his weapons, and sometimes we'd shoot white phosphorus rockets to give him something to aim at. After two or three passes, he'd wait for our damage assessment before heading home.

Before its deployment in Operation *Desert Shield/Desert Storm*, it was alleged that the AH-64 would not be able to handle desert conditions, in spite of the fact that it had been tested on exercise in Egypt and had coped with the all-pervading sand. In the event, it proved to be highly effective in the Gulf. (DOD)

Apaches were deployed to Saudi Arabia by sea, most coming from front line units in Germany. Flown to Dutch ports, they were loaded onto container ships for the three-week voyage east, where they were quickly reassembled and sent to forward operating bases close to the Iraqi border. (DOD)

While Apaches can self-deploy over long distances, they can also be shipped worldwide by air at very short notice. Here, an AH-64 Apache of the 4th Battalion, 3d Armored Cavalry Regiment, based at Ft Carson, Colorado, is winched down the ramp of an Air National Guard C-5 Galaxy at Eielson Air Force Base in Alaska, during Exercise Northern Edge 98. (DOD)

Peacekeeping

Since the end of the 1991 Gulf War, US Army Apaches have been involved in several peacekeeping efforts on behalf of NATO, the UN and other multinational coalitions. In the immediate aftermath of *Desert Storm*, during which the US Army's Apache had distinguished itself, the type was called back into action to support UN peacekeeping efforts in northern Iraq. As part of Operation *Provide Comfort*, the operation to protect Iraq's Kurd population from Saddam Hussein's army following an abortive uprising, AH-64As were deployed from the 6th Squadron, 6th Cavalry (the "Sixshooters"), part of the 11th Aviation Brigade, to Turkey. On April 24, 1991, the Apaches air-deployed from their base at Illesheim in Germany. They were then used to provide armed escort for UN transport helicopters flying supplies in to Kurdish refugee camps in the mountains of northern Iraq, and were particularly useful in deterring Iraqi army operations at night.

When the US Army finally entered the Balkans theater in December 1995, the deployment of the 1st Armored Division from its German

Apaches can work with tanks just as well as they can kill them. Here, M1A1 Abrams main battle tanks from the 1st Armored Division coordinate their fire with two AH-64A Apaches as they practice at a range in Glamoc, Bosnia-Herzegovina, on April 2, 1998. The tankers and the helicopters had been deployed to Bosnia-Herzegovina as part of the Stabilization Force in Operation *Joint Guard*. (DOD)

bases was spearheaded and protected by AH-64As from the 2/227th and 3/227th Attack Helicopter Battalions, normally based at Hanau. The Apaches deployed ahead of the main force, first to Taszar in Hungary where the US force was assembling, and then on to Zupanje in Croatia in order to protect engineers building a pontoon bridge over the River Sava. Finally, the Apaches settled at Tuzla.

As the lead element of IFOR (Implementation Force), the 1st Armored Division was involved in separating the warring factions in Bosnia. The Apaches were busy flying border patrols along the Zone of Separation in order to deter any infringements, and also escorted transport helicopters and ground convoys. They were used to provide security during many operations, including VIP visits.

In April 1996, elements of 6/6 Cavalry served as a part of Task Force Eagle for 7 months, under 1st Armored Division control. In October of 1996, Task Force 11, consisting of the Regimental Headquarters, 2d Battalion 6th Cavalry, 2d Battalion 1st Aviation Regiment and 7th Battalion, 159th Aviation Regiment, deployed to Bosnia-Herzegovina for eight months in support of Operation *Joint Endeavor* and Operation *Joint Guard*.

In June of 1998 the Regimental Headquarters, 6/6 Cavalry and elements of 5/158 Aviation were again deployed to Bosnia-Herzegovina for 5 months, in support of Operations *Joint Guard* and *Joint Forge*. The AH-64A's advanced sensors and sighting systems proved effective in detecting and tracking anti-government and pro-Serbian forces attempting to move by night. However, the Apache story has not been all about success, and the next major deployment to the Balkans would not be one to remember.

When NATO launched Operation *Allied Force* against Yugoslavia on March 24, 1999, there were no official plans to deploy Apaches. On April 4, however, the Pentagon announced that the attack helicopter would be deployed. Much fanfare surrounded this announcement, as many commanders and politicians had been calling for the type's use since the first days of the war. However, the deployment of Task Force Hawk, as the Apache force was known, was to be something of a public relations disaster.

Twenty-four AH-64As were deployed from the 11th Aviation Regiment's 2/6 Cavalry and 6/6 Cavalry at Illesheim. Supporting them were 26 UH-60L Black Hawks and CH-47D Chinooks (the latter to provide forward air refueling points), together with an armored and infantry force to ensure the Apache's protection on the ground. One source at the time suggested it would take 115 missions by C-17 to airlift the entire Task Force Hawk to its base at Rinas in Albania. In all, some 2,000 US soldiers were part of the initial deployment to Albania.

The Apaches were expected to arrive in eight to 14 days. Deployment got under way on April 14, but the Apaches were held up at Pisa in Italy for some days, before the first arrived at Tirana on April 21. By April 26 the Apaches were finally all in-country, but on that day one was lost when it hit a tree during a daylight training sortie.

Task Force Hawk had initially been directed to deploy to Macedonia, to use the existing facilities and local experience gained by US Army units based at Camp Able Sentry. Unfortunately, the Macedonian government would not agree to helicopters being based there and the deployment had to be shifted to Albania, where the government had agreed to accept them. The change in location necessitated the deployment of additional

A wave of US Army UH-60 Black Hawk and AH-64A Apache attack helicopters from Task Force Hawk comes in for a landing at Rinas Airport in Tirana, Albania, on April 25, 1999. The Task Force Hawk helicopters were deployed to Albania in support of NATO Operation *Allied Force*, directed against Serbian targets in the Federal Republic of Yugoslavia. In the event, they did not play any part in the campaign. (DOD)

protection and support units, as facilities were not as well established as in Macedonia.

At the time, Tirana airport was a "bare bones" facility and the Apaches had to share space with massive amounts of humanitarian aid pouring into Albania. Task Force Hawk was in competition with the humanitarian Task Force Shining Hope for scarce airbase resources. The airport remained a bottleneck despite efforts by Air Force engineers to expand its capacity.

Although the Task Force Hawk deployment involved only 24 helicopters, the actual operation involved much bigger resources. On April 20, 1999, Secretary of Defense William S. Cohen ordered the deployment of additional units to provide force protection for Task Force Hawk in Albania. This deployment brought the approximate number of US troops in Task Force Hawk to 3,300. Eventually, the total force deployed to support Task Force Hawk grew to more than 5,000 personnel.

In fact, Task Force Hawk was an Army Aviation Brigade Combat Team in all but name. In addition to the attack helicopter regiment with its Apaches, the Task Force included support helicopters, a corps aviation brigade headquarters, a corps artillery brigade headquarters with a Multiple-Launch Rocket System (MLRS) battalion, a ground maneuver brigade combat team, a corps support group, a signal battalion, a headquarters troop battalion, a military police detachment, a psychological operations detachment, and a special operations command-and-control element.

It took almost four weeks to deploy the Apaches. The Apache crews started training for deep strike missions against Serb forces in Kosovo. Given the changes in the scope and specifics of Task Force Hawk's deployment, a different means of moving the task force might have been chosen.

The first US troops to die in the NATO air offensive against Yugoslavia were two 11th Aviation Regiment aircrew, killed on May 4, 1999, in the crash of their Apache helicopter. The crash occurred about 47 miles northeast of the Tirana-Rinas Airport during a training mission in support of Operation *Allied Force*.

The Apache crews sent to Albania were not as experienced as they might have been. Nearly two thirds of the pilots and gunners had less

Ground crewmen load 30mm cannon rounds into an Apache's M230 30mm Chain Gun. Apaches have been and can be expected to be deployed to any climatic area from the desert to the Arctic: training in Alaska proved invaluable in dealing with the harsh conditions encountered in Balkan winters during peacekeeping operations. (DOD)

than 500 hours of Apache flight time when they arrived. Very few were qualified to use night vision goggles (NVG). Albania, like much of the Balkans, is an extremely rugged country not very well mapped and with poorly marked power lines and other dangerous features. As a result, it was not a good place to rely solely on forward-looking infrared sensors in night operations. This was one of the main reasons for the delays in declaring the Apaches combat ready, since a thorough NVG training program had to be established during the early stages of deployment. Pilots also expressed some dissatisfaction with the APR-39 radar warning system, the APR-136 jammer, and lacked confidence in the ALQ-144 IR jammer's true capabilities.

Another problem came when the attack helicopters were integrated with tactical aircraft for air tasking. Coordinating rotary-wing aircraft operations into the Air Tasking Order proved difficult, because this mission was not covered in current Army doctrine, nor was it exercised on a regular basis in joint training. As a result, the Services had to work through numerous complexities associated with the evolution of new missions and employment concepts for Army helicopters, radars, artillery, and other assets in the middle of a major conflict. In fact, the tactics, techniques, or procedures required for this mission had not yet been developed when Operation *Allied Force* took place.

As Operation *Allied Force* progressed and the effectiveness of the ongoing campaign became evident, it was decided not to add Task Force Hawk's firepower to the air operation. NATO did not use the Apaches because the situation had changed between the time they were requested and when they were combat ready. By the time the helicopters were ready, many of the tanks that would have been killed by the Apaches were dispersed into villages and even individual homes. Even with the Apache's precision attack capability, going after the tanks could well have resulted in heavy civilian casualties. Training continued, but the Allied Force air operations ceased on June 9 without the much-heralded Task Force Hawk having ever fired a shot in anger.

However, on the following day, a dozen 6/6 Cavalry Apaches deployed forward to Camp Able Sentry at Petrovec in Macedonia in preparation for *Joint Guardian*, the operation to occupy Kosovo following the Serb withdrawal. Known as Task Force 12, the Apaches were the first NATO helicopters to cross into Kosovo, on June 12, scouting ahead and then escorting the British Pumas and Chinooks that were taking in the first troops. Escort and policing missions were flown throughout the short duration insertion operation.

A: AH-64A Apache

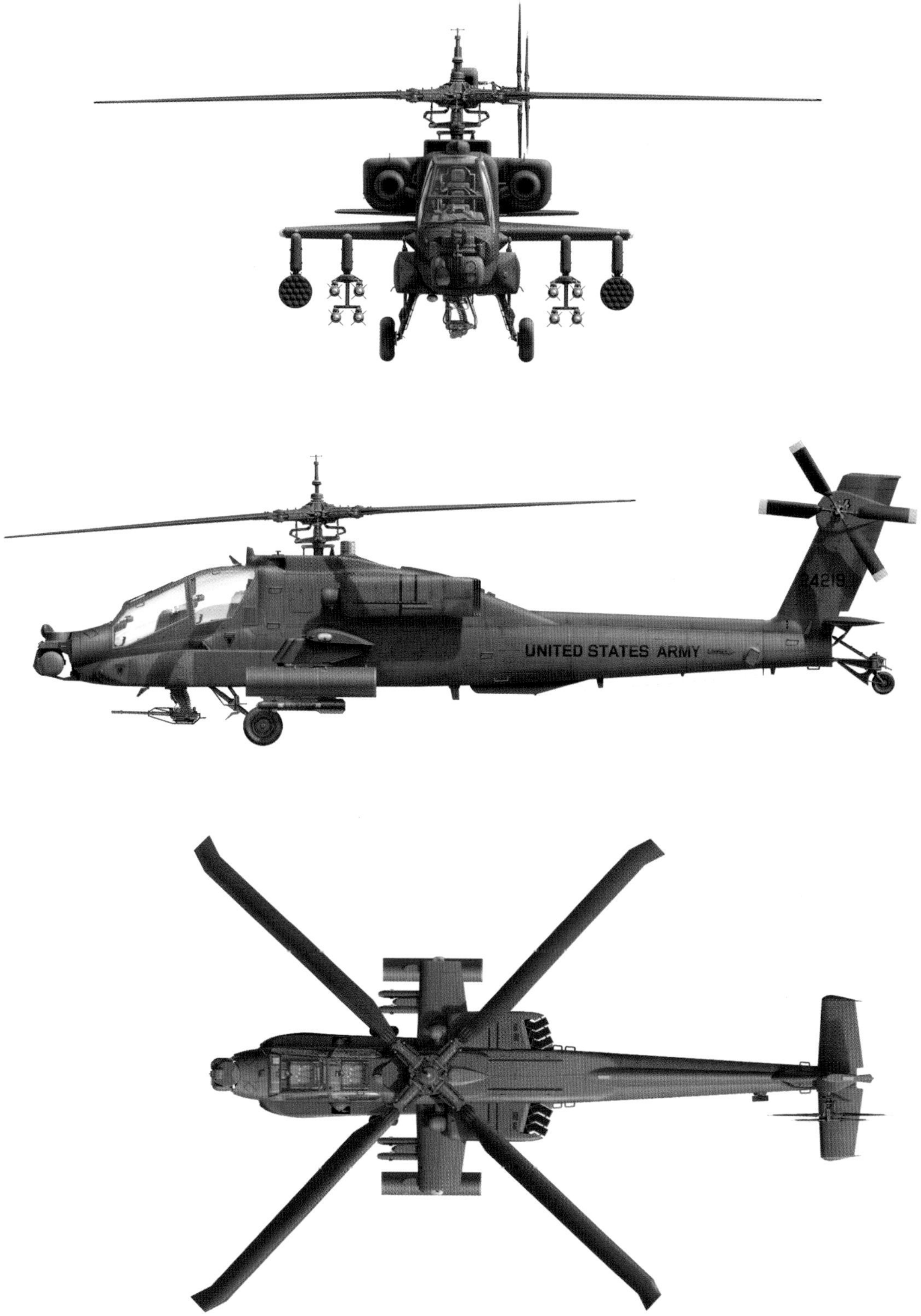

A

B1: YAH-64 profile

B2: Early AH-64A profile (without armament)

B

C: AH-64A in the Gulf

c

D: AH-64D

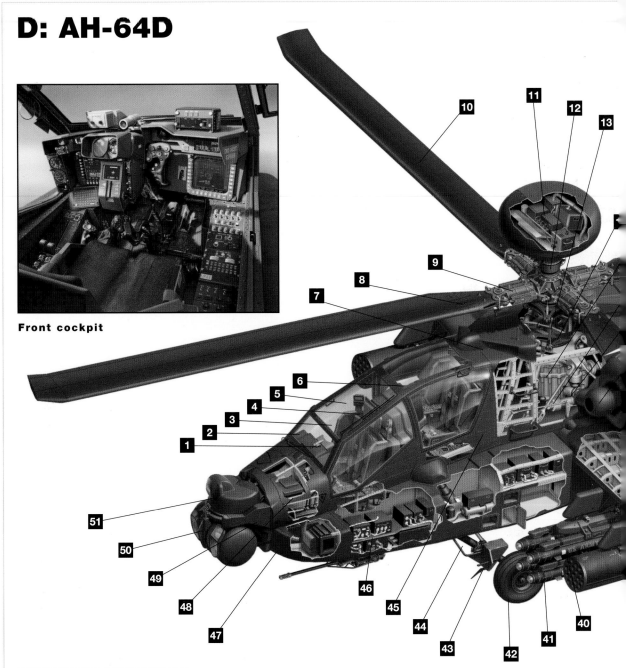

Front cockpit

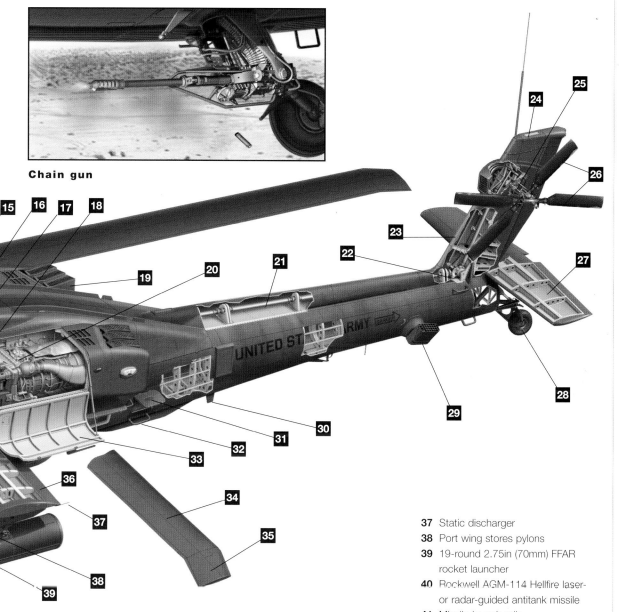

Chain gun

15 16 17 18

19 20 21 22 23 24 25 26 27 28 29 30 31 32 33 34 35 36 37 38 39

UNITED STATES ARMY

37 Static discharger
38 Port wing stores pylons
39 19-round 2.75in (70mm) FFAR
   rocket launcher
40 Rockwell AGM-114 Hellfire laser-
   or radar-guided antitank missile
41 Missile launch rails
42 Main wheel
43 Boarding step
44 Main landing gear leg
45 Cockpit ventilating air louvre
46 Port avionics equipment bay
47 Fuselage sponson fairing
48 Nose electronics compartment
49 TADS/PNVS Swivelling turret
50 Target Acquisition and
   Designation System (TADS)
51 Pilot's Night Vision System
   (PNVS)

21 Tail rotor transmission shaft
22 Bevel drive intermediate gearbox
23 Tail fin/rotor pylon
24 Fin tip aerial/radar warning fairing
25 Tail rotor hub
26 Asymmetric tail rotor blades
27 Tailplane
28 Castoring tail wheel

29 Chaff and flare dispenser
30 UHF aerial
31 Access hatch
32 Handgrips/maintenance steps
33 Engine access hatch
34 Fiberglass main rotor skin
35 Swept main rotor blade tip
36 Port stub wing

F: AH-64D in Afghanistan

F

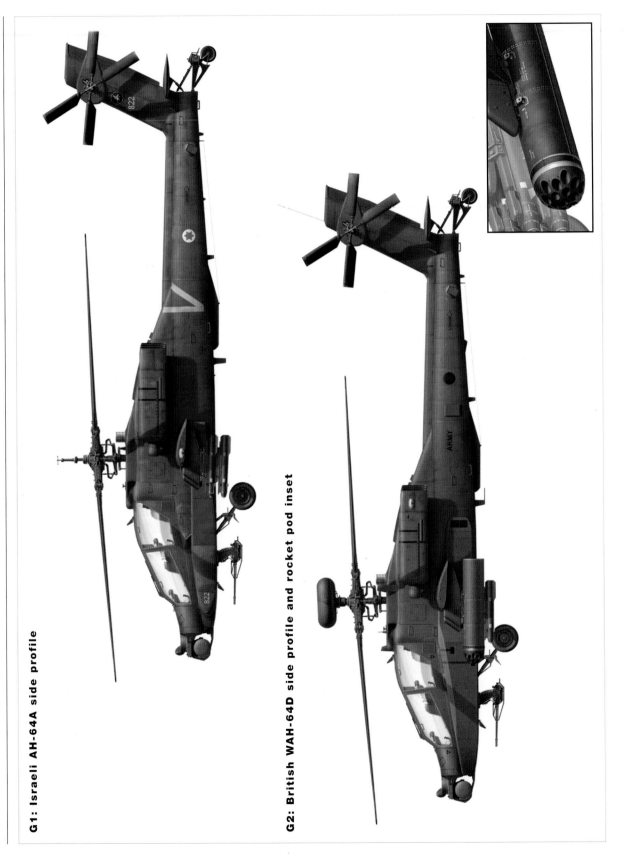

G1: Israeli AH-64A side profile

G2: British WAH-64D side profile and rocket pod inset

G

Apaches took center stage in the operations that followed, proving extremely useful in patrolling and policing areas where ethnic violence continued. In several instances, Albanian terrorists gave themselves up when confronted with a hovering Apache. In December 1999 the force moved to Camp Bondsteel in Kosovo. By this time the original 6/6 Cavalry aircraft had been replaced by eight from B Company, 1/1 Aviation "Wolfpack" and also six Apaches from the United Arab Emirates Air Force's 69th Air Combat Group.

Late in the year 2000, Apaches embarked on another peacekeeping operation, marking the first operational deployment for the AH-64D and the first for the Apaches of the Royal Netherlands Air Force. Four aircraft were deployed from Gilze-Rijen air base to the French colonial outpost of Djibouti, from where they have assisted UN forces in policing the uneasy ceasefire between Ethiopia and Eritrea. Four Dutch CH-47D Chinooks were also used, remaining in the area into 2001.

Afghanistan

In 2001, US Army Apaches were sent to Afghanistan to take part in the campaign against Al Qaeda and the Taleban.

On March 1, 2002, five 101st Airborne Division Apaches were assigned to Operation *Anaconda*. This was a major search and destroy action in eastern Afghanistan, whose aim was to winkle out hold-out Taleban and Al Qaeda fighters from their deeply dug-in positions in mountains. Another Apache arrived later in the morning, and a seventh flew up from Kandahar to join the fight the first afternoon.

The fighting was fierce and, with Al Qaeda fighters so close to US troops, close air support from "fast mover" jets was often out of the question. The Apache helicopters provided the most responsive close air support for forces taking heavy fire from the Al Qaeda hideouts in the initial days of the battle.

"The weapon that changed the face of the battle for us was the Apache," said Colonel Frank Wiercinski, commander of the 101st Airborne Division (Air Assault)'s 3d Brigade, who was in charge of all conventional US troops in the battle. In an after-action interview he continued:

Apaches deployed to Afghanistan in relatively small numbers and were used in a variety of offensive and escort roles. Here, four UH-60 Black Hawks are transporting six US congressmen during an operational overview tour of operations in Iraq and Afghanistan. Two AH-64D Apaches are just lifting off to provide close escort. (USCENTCOM)

I was just so impressed by its capability. I had never seen the Apache in combat before, though I've always trained with it. I am a firm believer right now that a brigade combat team commander needs his Apache battalion in an air assault division – its ability to protect us en route, its ability to set the conditions on the landing zones and then its close combat attack capability to take out fires.

Artillery is a wonderful asset, but you need an observer, you need a sensor, and then you've got the artillery tube as the shooter. An Apache can do all of that, and it's always moving.

On station in the valley from dawn on the battle's first day, the Apaches flew again and again through withering small-arms, heavy machine-gun and rocket-propelled grenade fire to provide fire support to the beleaguered infantry troops.

The Apache's toughness came into its own that day. Any other helicopters would have been shot out of the sky; while five out of the seven were non-mission-capable by the end of the first day, they got their crews home. A testament to the ferocity of the ground fire is the fact that 27 out of the 28 rotor blades on the seven helicopters were pierced by bullets and shrapnel. Most were repaired, and the Apaches continued to support the operation. The sweep by more than 2,000 US, Afghan and other coalition forces through the valleys and over the mountains south of Gardez denied surviving Al Qaeda and Taleban forces use of that remote area, with its many caves, as a base of operations.

Even without hostile action, Afghanistan is hard on helicopters. Penetrating dust clogs everything from the Teflon bearings that help tilt the rotors to the "disco balls" – high-tech jamming devices – on the fuselage. Crews must run water through the Apache's engines after ten hours of operation to prevent moving parts from jamming solid. Altitude does not help, either. Bagram, the main base near Kabul, lies nearly a mile above sea level, and the thinner air reduces the capacity of all helicopters. The lifting capacity of the big CH-47 Chinook transport helicopters was reduced by 10,000lb, and the Apaches could barely make it over some of the 12,000ft mountains, even with the bigger engines they were given before the war. In operations, the rotors kick up a hurricane of dust, making it hard to find the ground during landings. However, mechanics say that despite some added maintenance, most helicopters in Afghanistan have served surprisingly well. One Apache managed 1,300 flight hours in a month – three times what a US-based helicopter normally flies.

Apaches continue to serve and fight in Afghanistan. In June 2003, coalition forces returned to the Shahi Kot mountain range for the first time since Operation *Anaconda*. Operation *Dragon Fury* could be considered part two of Operation *Anaconda*, intended to root out Al Qaeda and anti-coalition militias suspected of still operating in the valley near the Afghanistan–Pakistan border. Some 500 troops, including 150 Italians and 20 aircraft, were involved in the two-day operation in Paktia province. In a briefing after the action, Air Force Lieutenant Colonel Douglas Lefforge spoke to reporters at the Bagram Airbase:

Early on Monday morning and through yesterday, the coalition Task Force Devil conducted offensive operations in the Shahi Kot region in the Paktia province to prevent the re-emergence of terrorism, deny anti-coalition members sanctuary, and prevent further attacks against non-governmental organizations, coalition forces and equipment.

Objectives included defeating or capturing ACMs (anti-coalition members) operating in the Shahi Kot region, establishing blocking positions to prevent ACMs from escaping from the Shahi Kot Valley and destroying or recovering ACM weapons and ammunition.

UH-60 Black Hawks, CH-47 Chinooks and AH-64 Apache helicopters on the mission were supported by fixed-wing aircraft, but there were no reports of fighting. One AH-64 Apache helicopter crashed during the operation but the incident was believed to be an operational accident rather than a result of enemy fire.

The most recent addition to the Apache force in Afghanistan came on April 1, 2004, when six Royal Netherlands Air Force AH-64D Apaches deployed to Kabul. From their first week of operations they came under hostile fire but at the time of writing had suffered no serious damage.

Operation *Iraqi Freedom*

On March 19, 2003, a US-led coalition attacked Saddam Hussein's Iraq in an attempt to halt the proliferation of weapons of mass destruction in the volatile Middle East. The war began with a "decapitation" attack on a suspected gathering of Iraqi national leaders in Baghdad. Coalition air forces also struck at long-range artillery emplacements, air defense sites and surface-to-surface missile sites.

The next day, the ground war began. The 3d Infantry Division (Mechanized) rolled into southern Iraq at 0600 local time, meeting only slight resistance. Special operation forces went into action throughout western and southern Iraq. The 1st Marine Expeditionary Force and British forces also crossed into Iraq to seize and protect southern Iraq's oil fields.

AH-64As and AH-64D Longbows were powerful assets in the fast-moving "major combat" phase of Operation *Iraqi Freedom*, with an estimated 140 aircraft in the theater of operations. The Apaches that

Members of the 101st Airborne Division converse on the flight line shortly before flying across the border into Iraq on March 23, 2003. The division's heavily laden UH-60 and CH-47 transports will be escorted on the operation by the AH-64 Apache helicopters seen waiting to be armed on the ramp. (DOD)

Smoke and flames engulf an Iraqi antiaircraft gun and its towing vehicle following a strike from an AH-64 Apache on Sunday March 23, 2003. The Iraqis had learned some lessons from the previous Gulf War: their vehicles did not line up en masse as previously, but operated in a widely dispersed fashion. (DOD)

had been committed to Operation *Enduring Freedom* in Afghanistan had more powerful T700-GE-701C engines to match the performance challenges of the mountainous terrain. These engines also provided sufficient power for the mission profiles flown by the Longbow Apache in *Iraqi Freedom*. The integral inlet air particle separator of the T700 engine proved effective in the dense dust, and the Army quickly fielded a successful Tactical Engine Wash System (TEWS).

AH-64Ds of the 1st Battalion, 3d Aviation Regiment, 3d Infantry Division used the radar-guided AGM-114L Hellfire missile for the first time in combat in attacking an Iraqi observation post on the Kuwaiti border. At the night mission's outset, an AH-64D flew into a sand dune dodging ground fire, but later lifted itself off and returned to base. The 1st of the 3d also made the first tank kill with the radar-guided Hellfire. As they did in *Desert Storm*, Apaches in Iraqi Freedom devastated massed armor. When asked why he surrendered his unit, an Iraqi Republican Guard general reportedly responded simply, "Apaches."

The conventional combat portion of the invasion of Iraq was over quickly, and US and Allied forces quickly found themselves in a very different counter-insurgency war. Here, an AH-64D Apache Longbow helicopter provides air support for combat engineers as they clear an area following the detonation of an improvised explosive device. (DOD)

AH-64s in Operation *Iraqi Freedom* nevertheless fought a different kind of battle than they had 12 years before. Iraqi tanks in 2003 were generally dispersed, with air defenses hidden in cities or in civilian areas. Apache crews learned to use more flexible tactics in the changing fight. The 1st of the 3d transitioned from massed deep strike tactics to continuous close combat using small teams of Apaches. While lead crews attacked targets from standoff ranges, wingmen protected the shooters from close-in threats. Shoot-on-the-move tactics also got the Apache out of its vulnerable tank-killing hover.

The ground threat was greater than in *Desert Storm*. With tanks as bait, the Iraqis set ambushes with RPGs, mortars and other infantry weapons. The much-publicized deep strike near Karbala in March left 31 Apaches damaged by RPGs and gunfire and gave Iraq a very public victory. Two Americans were captured and a sophisticated US Army helicopter left in Iraqi hands, eventually to be destroyed by a USAF strike.

In March 2003 one Apache Longbow was downed and 14 others were shot up outside Baghdad after facing a hail of small-arms fire from the ground. The Iraqis were waiting for the Longbows. They used cell phones to give advance notice to the troops, who were told: "As soon as you hear them, fill the sky with lead." In spite of the increased threat, three Apache squadrons destroyed up to 50 vehicles and artillery pieces during the battle for Baghdad.

On June 12, 2003, an Apache belonging to the Army's 101st Airborne Division was shot down near the town of Duluiyah, north of Baghdad. Both crew members were rescued. On January 13, 2004, an Apache was shot down near the western Iraqi town of Habbaniyah. This was the second of the heavily armed gun-ships downed by guerrilla fire since President Bush declared an end to major combat on May 1, 2003. On Easter Sunday, April 11, 2004, an AH-64 Apache helicopter was downed by ground fire in the morning, during fighting in western Baghdad, killing its two crew members.

The adverse headlines which followed these losses ignored the repeated message that the Apache could take punishment and return to the fight. One AH-64A from 2/6 Cavalry took multiple hits during the push for the Iraqi capital. The pilot withdrew to an aid station to get his wounded co-pilot/gunner bandaged, patched up the aircraft with tape and epoxy and rejoined the battle.

APACHE OPERATORS

US Army

The first handover of an Apache to the US Army took place on January 26, 1984, although this was only a formality since the heavily instrumented aircraft concerned would remain with Hughes/McDonnell Douglas. In fact, it was not until the delivery of PV-13 that a US Army crew could fly an Apache away and call it their own. Initial deliveries were made to US Army Training and Doctrine Command bases at Ft Eustis, Virginia (home of the Army logistics school), and Ft Rucker, Alabama (the US Army's center of flying training). Apache acquisition ultimately amounted to: 138 (FY85),

The first US Army unit to become operational with the Apache was the 7th Battalion, 17th Cavalry Brigade at Ft Hood. However, long before it achieved its initial operational capability, Apaches had been in service at Army training schools at Ft Eustis and at Ft Rucker. (TRH Pictures)

The stealthiest and most capable combat helicopter ever built, the Boeing-Sikorsky RAH-66 Comanche was intended to supplement and then replace the Apache. However, the end of the Cold War meant that its incredible capabilities were simply too expensive for the lower-intensity conflicts that are likely in the foreseeable future. (Boeing)

116 (FY86), 101 (FY87), 77 (FY88), 54 (FY89), 154 (FY90) and a follow-on batch of 10 (FY95), for a grand total of 827 AH-64A Apaches (including six prototypes and 171 acquired in the first half of the 1980s). The first unit to convert to the Apache was the 7th Battalion, 17th Cavalry Brigade at Ft Hood, which began its 90-day battalion-level conversion in April 1986. The last of the 821 AH-64As destined for the US Army was delivered on April 30, 1996. This was the 915th production Apache.

In December 1995, US Army Aviation launched the transition of its Apache fleet from AH-64A to AH-64D Longbow Apache standard, when it signed an initial production deal with McDonnell Douglas (now Boeing) to rebuild and upgrade 18 aircraft as its first batch of Longbow Apaches. The following year, in September 1996, the Army completed a major five-year remanufacturing agreement for the supply of 232 AH-64Ds. During early 1997 the first two AH-64D prototype aircraft were deployed to Ft Irwin, California, to participate in the Army's Force XXI field exercise – the centerpiece of US Army efforts to rethink its tactics, techniques, and procedures for combat in the 21st century.

McDonnell Douglas delivered the first "production" AH-64D for the Army on schedule, on March 31, 1997 (following its first flight on March 17). By April 4, 1998, all 24 aircraft from the first AH-64D production batch had been delivered and, later that month, seven aircraft entered service with the Army's lead Longbow Apache unit, the 1st Battalion, 227th Aviation Regiment (1/227th), 1st Cavalry Division, based at Ft Hood, Texas. After a period of eight months of intensive company and battalion-level training, the US Army's first Longbow Apache combat battalion was certified as operationally ready on November 9, 1998. All AH-64D training, from individual to battalion level, is conducted at Ft Hood by the newly reconstituted 21st Cavalry Brigade. The Army's second Longbow Apache battalion – the 2d Battalion, 101st Aviation Regiment, based at Ft Campbell Kentucky – was certified as combat-ready on November 2, 1999.

Final negotiations for the remanufacture of a second batch of 298 Longbow Apaches were launched in 1999 and, on December 9 that year, Boeing (which had taken over McDonnell Douglas in August 1997) delivered the 100th AH-64D to the US Army. In September 1999, four years after work began on the AH-64A remanufacturing program, Boeing signed a contract to provide the Army with a follow-on batch of 269 AH-64Ds, from 2002 to 2006. This second five-year deal would provide a total of 501 Longbow Apaches for Army Aviation, with around 150 already delivered at that point.

By the beginning of 2004, nine US Army Apache Longbow battalions had been certified as combat ready. In June 2004, the Army's tenth Longbow unit, 2/6 Cavalry Brigade, based in Illesheim, Germany, completed its training cycle at Ft Hood. The unit fought in Iraq in 2003 as an AH-64A Apache battalion. Upon their return, the helicopters were returned to the Boeing factory at Mesa, AZ, where they were remanufactured into next-generation AH-64D Apache Longbows.

Of the ten Longbow battalions deployed, six are based in the United States and four are based overseas. On October 16, 2001, the first US Army AH-64Ds to be deployed abroad arrived in Seoul, South Korea, opening a new chapter in American Longbow operations. The aircraft, all from the newly re-equipped 1st Battalion, 2d Aviation Regiment, were transported to Korea by sea and then reassembled. Until 1999, when it began its AH-64D conversion, the 1st Battalion had been an AH-64A unit.

Sixteen US Army National Guard (ANG) and two Reserve units are flying or expect to receive AH-64 Apaches. Three ANG units – Arizona, South Carolina, and Idaho – and Reserve units in Kentucky and Texas that fly AH-64A Apache helicopters are transitioning to the AH-64D Apache Longbow. The Army National Guard would like to convert the other 13 units to Longbow standard.

The cancellation of the Comanche program means that the Apache will remain the sharp edge of US Army offensive capability well into the 21st century. Currently the busiest user of Apaches is US Central Command, which controls AH-64Ds in both Afghanistan and in Iraq. (USCENTCOM)

New organization

In recent years US Army Aviation has undergone a series of operational transformations that have had a significant effect on the way its Apache force is organized. During the 1990s, the Aviation Restructuring Initiative (ARI) saw a reduction in the number of Apache units, but an increase in the strength of the surviving battalions from 18 to 24 aircraft. The ARI was successfully implemented but in March 2000 the Army announced a completely new Aviation Force Modernization Plan (AFMP), driven by the need to move away from single-purpose combat units to a more flexible, multi-purpose organization, the prospect of the extremely advanced Boeing-Sikorsky RAH-66 Comanche entering service, and the wider availability of the AH-64D.

The AH-64D Apache Longbow made its first overseas deployment, to Korea, in 2001. Here, on June 5, 2003, a newly delivered Longbow from the 3d Squadron, 6th Cavalry, is test-flown over Pusan harbor and certified as airworthy before it flies to the squadron's base of Camp Humphreys. (DOD)

It was intended that each US Army corps organization would be allocated one Combat Brigade and one Combat Support Brigade. These new "Objective Force" Combat Brigades were to consist of a Multi-Functional Battalion with 10 AH-64Ds (i.e. one company), 10 RAH-66 Comanches and 10 UH-60s. However, until the RAH-66 entered service the Corps instead would operate with a temporary Transitional Force Combat Brigade structure with 16 AH-64s (two companies) and one company of UH-60s. The AFMP also reorganized the Army's divisional aviation assets. Each of the 18 currently established divisions (active and reserve) was to have two Multi-Functional Battalions (10 AH-64Ds, 10 RAH-66s and up to 20 UH-60s), plus a Divisional Cavalry Squadron. Again, a Transitional Force was to be equipped with eight AH-64Ds, eight OH-58Ds and 16 UH-60s, before the final Objective Force levels would have been available in 2010.

Everything changed in February 2004, when the Army stopped all further development of the RAH-66 Comanche. Far and away the most capable combat helicopter ever built, the stealthy Comanche had been designed to fight in a Cold War environment, and was over-equipped for the kind of expeditionary war emerging in the 21st century. The Apache, especially the AH-64D Longbow, is more than capable of flying attack missions into the foreseeable future, so the Comanche has become an expensive luxury. Reassigning the $15 billion cost of the program will allow the Army to acquire more UH-60 transport helicopters as well as a new scout helicopter to replace the OH-58, and more of the Apache force can be brought up to Longbow standard and beyond.

The first upgraded Block II Apaches were delivered to the US Army in February 2003. Block II aircraft include upgrades to the digital communications systems to improve communications within the "tactical internet." Block III upgrades, intended for introduction from 2008, will include more digital equipment and a new composite rotor blade. Block III Apaches will also have the ability to control unmanned aerial vehicles.

Foreign operators

With the role of the dedicated battlefield helicopter steadily increasing in importance in the 1970s and 1980s, it came as no surprise to McDonnell Douglas to find that, despite its initially high purchase price, there was considerable interest in the Apache from overseas operators. Following the first Gulf War, McDonnell Douglas received a flood of requests from countries interested in purchasing new Apaches to reinforce their attack forces. Their aims were to operate the helicopters in emerging local conflicts, which, although characterized as low-intensity combat, have become increasingly high-tech.

In September 2003 Greece agreed to purchase 12 next-generation AH-64D Apache Longbows, which it will add to its existing fleet of 20 AH-64A Apache combat helicopters like the one seen here. At the time of its original purchase, the Apache was seen by the Greeks as a weapon to counter a possible attack by fellow NATO member Turkey. (Aerospace Publishing)

Greece

Constant tension between Greece and Turkey over claimed territorial violations on both sides led Greece to upgrade its attack helicopter fleet. On December 24, 1991, Hellenic Army Aviation finalized its order for 12 AH-64As, with an option for eight more examples, which could then be increased by a further four. Delivered by sea in June 1995, a total of 20 Apaches is now in service with 1 Tagma Epidolkon Elikopteron (attack helicopter battalion), based at Stefanovikon. In September 2003, Greece contracted with Boeing to buy a further 12 AH-64Ds.

Netherlands

Filling a requirement for a multi-role armed helicopter to undertake escort, reconnaissance, protection, and fire-support missions, the Apache proved to be the clear choice for the Netherlands. Despite objections from economic affairs advisers, the Netherlands announced its decision in favor of the AH-64D Apache on May 24, 1995, and so became the first export customer for this variant. To gain experience with the type, 12 AH-64As were leased from the US Army from November 13, 1996, till February 19, 2001. Thirty AH-64Ds were delivered from 1998, without the mast-mounted Longbow radar. The Apaches form the centerpiece of the newly evolving Dutch rapid-deployment Air Mobile Brigade. Six AH-64D are based at Ft Hood in Texas for flight and weapons training. In January 2004 it was reported that 6 AH-64Ds were up for sale.

United Kingdom

The United Kingdom's search for an attack helicopter became a priority during the mid-1980s, with approximately 127 aircraft being sought.

With an Invitation to Tender (ITT) issued in February 1993, the AH-64D became the clear favorite over the rival RAH-66A Comanche and BAe/Eurocopter Tiger. In an announcement made on July 13, 1995, the Apache was selected as the new attack helicopter for the Army Air Corps (AAC). Assembled by Westland as the WAH-64D, the Westland Apache (British Army designation AH Mk1) is powered by Rolls-Royce/Turbomeca RTM322 turboshafts, maintaining a commonality with the Royal Navy's EH101 Merlin. A reduced order for just 68 Apaches was eventually placed, and British Apaches will be equipped with the Shorts Helstreak air-to-air missile. With initial crew training taking place at Ft Rucker, the first Apache unit is No. 671 Squadron based at Middle Wallop in Hampshire. By the beginning of 2002, 18 WAH-64s had been delivered with another 41 arriving through the year. The final eight were delivered in 2003. The first WAH-64 squadron became operational in 2004 – the in-service target date having slipped dramatically from December 1998.

Middle East customers

A number of Arab clients have also placed orders for the AH-64 Apache. The United Arab Emirates Air Force received its first AH-64 Apache at a handover ceremony in Abu Dhabi on October 3, 1993, with deliveries continuing throughout the year. Twenty aircraft are based at Al Dhafra, and a further ten Apaches have since been delivered.

Saudi Arabia received 12 AH-64As in 1993 for its Army Aviation Command, based at King Khalid Military City. The Apaches operate alongside Bell 406CS Combat Scouts in hunter-killer teams. Saudi Army Aviation wants another 12 AH-64Ds, and would like to upgrade its earlier aircraft to the same standard.

Egypt received a $318 million arms package from the US in March 1995. This included 36 AH-64As, four spare Hellfire launchers, 34 rocket pods, six additional T700 engines, and one spare optical and laser turret. An additional 12 Apaches were also requested. All aircraft were to be of the latest US Army standard, with embedded GPS, but with a localized radio fit. Egypt plans to upgraded its force to AH-64D standard. The Egyptian Apaches are believed to have been allocated to the air force's single attack helicopter regiment.

The oil-rich Gulf States are among the few smaller nations wealthy enough to afford such an expensive helicopter as the Apache. One of the first overseas users of the type was the Air Force of the United Arab Emirates, which took delivery of the first of 20 Apaches in 1993. (Aerospace Publishing)

Other operators

Kuwait's requirements for a new attack helicopter led to its decision to acquire the AH-64 Apache. Japan has ordered 50 Longbow Apaches, while Singapore has bought eight AH-64Ds. Bahrain and the Republic of Korea expressed interest in acquiring the AH-64, although both deals have fallen through.

Israel

By far the most active of the non-American Apache users has been Israel, although there has been little released about its activities by the notoriously close-mouthed Israeli Defense Force. The first AH-64As (given the local name *Peten* or "Cobra") reached Israel in September 1990. Re-formed on September 12, 1990, Israel's No. 113 Squadron became the country's first operational Apache unit. In August/September 1993, Israel received a further 24 AH-64As (plus two UH-60As) from surplus US Army Europe stocks, as a "thank you" for support during Operation *Desert Storm*. All were delivered by C-5 from Ramstein Air Force Base. The arrival of these aircraft led to the establishment of the IDF/AF's second AH-64 squadron.

In early 2000 the IDF announced its intention to convert 12 of its AH-64As to AH-64D Apache Longbow standard. The deal would have cost the Israeli Air Force $400 million, with an option for 12 more helicopters to undergo the conversion as well. Upon entering office in April 2000, however, the new IAF Commander, Dan Halutz, ordered a re-evaluation of the conversion program, opting for the purchase of brand new AH-64Ds instead. The value of the program, which includes aircraft, ordnance, spares, training, and support is valued at $500 million. Plans to upgrade older A model Apaches have not been completely abandoned and several IDF Apaches may be upgraded by Boeing yet.

During November 1991, Israel became the first foreign AH-64 operator to use its aircraft in combat, when Hizbollah targets in southern Lebanon were hit in reprisal for guerrilla attacks against Israeli troops occupying the region. Sporadic operations continued over the next few years, including an attack on February 16, 1992, against the convoy carrying Hizbollah's Secretary General, Abbas Musawi. In 1996 Operation *Grapes of Wrath*, a major anti-guerrilla offensive into southern Lebanon,

Known as the *Peten* or "Cobra" in Israeli service, the AH-64 is operated by two squadrons of the IDF/AF, although only No.113 Squadron has been acknowledged by the notoriously close-mouthed Israeli Defense Force. (Aerospace Publishing)

was launched. Apaches led off the assault with a precision strike against a Hizbollah headquarters in southern Beirut, and were heavily used throughout the fighting.

Early in 2000 the simmering conflict flared up again ahead of the Israeli withdrawal from southern Lebanon. Again Apaches were in the thick of the action, attacking Hizbollah forces that had been firing over the border into Israel, and flying missions in support of the Israel-backed South Lebanon Army. On May 24 the last Israeli troops left Lebanese soil.

The *Peten* fleet has subsequently seen continued employment on retaliatory strikes across the border and into the West Bank and Gaza. Initially, targets such as Palestinian Authority police stations were singled out. Because of their urban locations, such missions required pinpoint attacks to minimize collateral damage and civilian fatalities. The AH-64, with its precision capability and AGM-114K Hellfire missiles, is better suited for such missions than conventional ground attack aircraft. However, in spite of its accuracy, more recent attacks against the homes of the organizations behind Palestinian suicide bombers have caused significant civilian casualties.

BIBLIOGRAPHY

Adcock, Al, *AH-64 Apache in Action*, Squadron Signal Publications, Texas, 1989

Bernstein, Jonathan, and Jim Laurier (illustrator), *AH-64 Apache Units of Operations Enduring Freedom & Iraqi Freedom*, Osprey Publishing, Oxford, 2005

Bradin, James W., *From Hot Air to Hellfire: The History of Army Attack Aviation*, Ballantine Books Inc, New York, 1994

Colucci, Frank, *Aero Series: The McDonnell Douglas Apache*, Vol. 33, TAB Books, Pennsylvania, 1987

Donald, David, and Jon Lake, *Encyclopedia of World Military Aircraft*, Aerospace Publishing/Barnes and Noble, London/New York, 2000

Gunston, Bill, *AH-64 Apache*, Osprey Publishing, London, 1986

Hewson, Robert, *World Air Power Journal* Volume 29, 'AH-64A/D Apache & AH-64D Longbow Apache', Aerospace Publishing, London, 1997

Monson, Lyle, and Kenneth Peoples, *Minigraph 18: McDonnell Douglas (Hughes) AH-64 Apache*, Aerofax Inc, Texas, 1987

Munro, Bob, *McDonnell Douglas AH-64 Apache*, Gallery Books, New York,1991

Peacock, Lindsay, and Doug Richardson, *Combat Aircraft: AH-64 Apache*, Salamander Books, London, 1992

Richardson, Doug, *Modern Fighting Aircraft AH 64*, Prentice Hall, New York, 1987

Jane's All the World's Aircraft, Jane's Information Group, Surrey, 1985–2005

COLOR PLATE COMMENTARY

A: AH-64A APACHE

This AH-64A Apache is one of those delivered to the 6th Cavalry Brigade, Air Combat, based at Ft Hood in Texas in the late 1980s. A typical Apache brigade at that time operated with three AH-64A battalions, each operating 18 aircraft. Overall color of the Apache is Aircraft Type 1 Green, formulated from chemically resistant polyurethane, while both tail and main rotor blades are painted flat matt black. This color scheme, together with the extreme low-visibility serial number, national markings, and unit identification, has remained constant through the Apache's operational career to date. Effective in a European-type environment, the dark colors make the Apache stand out rather more than might be desired in a desert or a winter environment, but it has not been considered necessary to develop specialist color schemes for varied terrains and climates.

The aircraft is designed to resist heavy machine-gun fire, and the crew compartment and key mechanical components, including the rotor blades, are designed to resist strikes from 23mm explosive cannon shells.

B1: YAH-64 PROFILE

The second Hughes YAH-64 prototype, and the first to fly, was AV-02 (Air Vehicle 02). Its first free hover took place on September 30, 1975, piloted by Hughes company test pilots Robert Perry and Raleigh Fletcher. All of the prototypes were minimally equipped, with basic flight instruments only. In this early form the aircraft did not carry the TADS/PNVS (Target Acquisition and Designation System/Pilot's Night Vision System) under the nose, and the nose itself had not yet been developed into its final form. The high "T" tail was found to cause nose pitch-up during slow nap-of-the-earth flight, reducing the forward visibility for the co-pilot/gunner, and the tailplane was repositioned on production models. The prototypes also lacked the Black Hole infrared suppression system

The Bell Model 409 or YAH-63 was the Apache's main competitor in the Army's AAH (Advanced Attack Helicopter) competition. Based on well-proven Huey Cobra principles, but essentially a new machine, it failed because the Army felt that the YAH-63's two-blade rotor was more vulnerable to damage than the Apache's four-bladed rotor, and it didn't like the YAH-63's tricycle landing gear. (TRH Pictures)

After starting the war with their attack on key Iraqi radar stations, the Apaches saw little action until the ground war started. In the short, vicious campaign, Apaches fired 2,876 Hellfire missiles, destroying over 1,300 Iraqi tanks, APCs, artillery pieces and other military vehicles. (Robert F. Dorr, Aerospace Publishing)

designed to cool engine exhaust. Then under development by Hughes, it was not yet ready for deployment, and the AV-series aircraft were flown with an interim fan-cooled system. Overall color carried by the prototype was a semi-gloss olive drab, with most other markings in black.

B2: EARLY AH-64A PROFILE (WITHOUT ARMAMENT)

The first production AH-64A, PV (Production Vehicle) 01, was rolled out in September 1983. The aircraft depicted here, AH-64A 83-23815, is from the second production batch. It is seen as it left the factory, prior to delivery to the US Army. This was the 40th aircraft off the production line (as indicated by the white "40" marking on the fuselage sponson).

One of the Apache's characteristics is its unusual tail rotor. Helicopters are inherently noisy, and much of that noise comes from their tail rotors. The distinctive tail rotor of the Apache is in fact a pair of two-bladed rotors, set at a 55-degree angle. This arrangement allows for more power to be developed at lower rotor speeds, and lower rotor speeds significantly reduce the helicopter's sound signature.

Replacing the original high "T" tailplane, the low-mounted, fully movable "stabilator" improved the poor low-level handling that had been encountered by the first prototypes. Other, less visible, improvements included an extended rotor mast and a slightly longer vertical fin.

C: AH-64A IN THE GULF

Apaches fighting in the first Gulf War had to operate through extremely hostile conditions. Desert dust is highly penetrating, and engine maintenance was vital to ensure the high level of serviceability demonstrated by the US Army's Apache force. Extremely high temperatures, plus a surprising amount of wet weather in the early months of 1991, added further challenges, but it was the Iraqi destruction of Kuwaiti oil facilities that added a unique series of problems. Burning oil wells covered the battlefield in a thick layer of black, greasy smoke, impairing visibility and adding peril to any kind of low-level flight. The Apache, with its sophisticated forward-looking infrared sensors incorporated into the PNVS (Pilot's Night Vision System), was

able to deal with the conditions better than most other combat aircraft in theater. It was able to destroy Iraqi vehicles from beyond their visual range: often, the first knowledge the Iraqis had that they were coming under attack was when Hellfire missiles, rockets, or 30mm cannon fire came blasting out of the murk.

D: AH-64D

The Apache Longbow is structurally very similar to the original AH-64A. Key improvements include a more powerful engine, improved avionics and navigation systems, and a modern digital cockpit. All AH-64Ds have received the improvements, but only 227 have been fitted with the Longbow radar.

The mast-mounted rotating antenna weighs some 250lb. It can scan through 360° in searching for aerial targets: in ground attack mode it can scan for vehicle and other non-flying targets over an arc of 270°. The AN/APG-78 Longbow radar can handle up to 256 targets simultaneously, presenting them to the pilot and gunner on color multifunction displays.

The AGM-114L Longbow missile is basically an AGM-114K Hellfire 2 with the semi-active laser seeker replaced by a millimetric radar seeker. Target acquisition is carried out by the Longbow Apache's Target Acquisition Designation Sight (TADS), which aligns the missile's onboard radar and inertial navigation system, and for moving or short-range targets the missile radar locks on before launch. Once launched, the missile's radar updates the missile's guidance system up to target impact.

ABOVE Soldiers perform maintenance on an AH-64 Apache attack helicopter on Forward Operating Base Speicher in Iraq. The aviation crew members are assigned to the 1st Infantry Division's 4th Brigade, which was deployed in support of Operation *Iraqi Freedom*. (DOD)

Desert flying in the Gulf brought its own unique hazards. The fine sand encountered in the region caused dangerous "brownouts:" the aircraft was enveloped by a thick cloud of rotor wash-blown sand on take off or landing. (McDonnell Douglas)

E: AH-64D

The AH-64 Apache is the US Army's heavy division/corps attack helicopter. The AH-64D Longbow remanufacture effort incorporates a millimeter wave fire control radar (FCR), radar frequency interferometer (RFI), fire-and-forget radar-guided Hellfire missile and cockpit management, and digitization enhancements. The combination of the FCR, RFI, and the advanced navigation and avionics suite of the aircraft provide increased situational awareness, lethality and survivability. Boeing is working closely with the US Army and its international customers to ensure the continued superiority of the Apache Longbow. Planned enhancements include a Modernized Target Acquisition Designation Sight/Pilot Night Vision Sensor, new digital communications systems, cognitive decision aiding, and connectivity with unmanned aerial vehicles. Apache Longbows have greater weapons accuracy at longer ranges and have the ability to fight more effectively at night and in nearly any weather. Apache's digital connectivity, powerful new sensors, individual weapon systems, advanced training devices, and maintenance support systems are all designed in anticipation of changing requirements and growth. US Army Apache Longbow production at The Boeing Company in Mesa will continue through at least 2006. The US Army has established programs designed to keep its Apaches at the leading edge of technology for the next 30-plus years.

F: AH-64D IN AFGHANISTAN

Helicopter operations in Afghanistan are dangerous – mountainous terrain offers insurgent ground troops the chance to engage slow-flying helicopters from close range with antiaircraft weapons, heavy machine guns and even antitank weapons. In Afghanistan, the height of the mountains means that helicopters are also operating close to their service ceilings, in very cold temperatures. Apaches in Afghanistan have flown racetrack patterns and running fire tactics, since at that altitude the helicopters have had insufficient power to hover. Constant movement also reduces vulnerability to ground fire: nevertheless, about 80 percent of AH-64s deployed have received some combat damage.

In spite of their vulnerability, US Army and Royal Netherlands Air Force Apaches provide NATO with a highly effective quick-reaction force. The Apaches can reach areas deep in the mountains that are inaccessible to conventional aircraft, and the helicopters can deliver precision attacks on enemy positions only yards from Allied ground troops.

G1: ISRAELI AH-64A SIDE PROFILE

In general, modern helicopters used by the Israeli Defense Forces have been painted a brown drab color, suitable for operations in the parched terrain of the Middle East. A notable exception is the AH-64 *Peten* ("Cobra," the local name applied to the Apache). Israeli AH-64s are painted in an all-over olive drab finish (although one Apache has been seen with an experimental light and dark sand color scheme). The paint is infrared suppressive, reducing the aircraft's heat signature in flight and so reducing its vulnerability to hostile heat-seeking missiles. For identification purposes at night the helicopters carry an infrared reflective "V"-shaped marking on the rear of the fuselage.

The first Israeli Air Force squadron to fly the AH-64 was No.113 "Hornet" or "Wasp" Squadron, which had formerly operated the Dassault Ouragan, IAI Nesher and IAI Kfir, and

Israeli AH-64s have seen extensive use in reprisal raids against Hizbollah and other Islamic groups seen as responsible for instigating suicide bomb attacks in Israel. Although the AH-64 is capable of greater precision than any other aerial attack platform, such raids necessarily cause some collateral damage, which often includes injuring or even killing innocent bystanders. (Aerospace Publishing)

which is credited with 52 enemy aircraft kills through its history. Re-formed on September 12, 1990, to operate the Apache, the squadron's identity has never been officially divulged, but the squadron's distinctive insignia painted onto Israeli AH-64s has been seen fairly regularly.

G2: BRITISH WAH-64D SIDE PROFILE AND ROCKET POD INSET

Sixty-seven Agusta Westland Apache AH Mk1s have been procured for the British Army. The aircraft is based on the Boeing (formerly McDonnell Douglas) AH-64D Apache Longbow that entered service with the US Army in 1998. Agusta Westland, the UK Prime Contractor, is building the aircraft to specific UK requirements, including a secure communications suite and a state-of-the-art Helicopter Integrated Defensive Aids System (HIDAS).

The first British Apaches, built by Boeing, were delivered in US Army standard Helicopter Green rather than the British Army's Helicopter Olive, but it is possible that in their operational service in the future British Apaches will be painted in the Army Air Corps' combat camouflage colors of olive drab and black. Although the weapon fit is much the same as on the American version of the Longbow, in place of the Hydra-70 rocket pods used by the US Army and others, British Apaches will carry the CRV-7 rocket pods designed by British Aerospace.

INDEX